Original Lyrics

By

Christian Passen

Lyrics Written by Christian Passen
Music Written by Christian Passen, Wayne
Bowers, and Eric Daugherty

Why is it I?

Potential Track List:

Track 1 – Misery
Track 2 – Dreamer
Track 3 – Taking Flight
Track 4 – Don't Let Me Down
Track 5 – Why is it I?
Track 6 – Reflections
Track 7 – Incomplete
Track 8 – How it has to be
Track 9 – Safety Net
Track 10 – Temporary

"MISERY"

Lyrics by Christian Passen
Music by Wayne Bowers

These once trusted eyes are so blind
I've searched long and hard to find
A love that was worth mine
But I'm tired and I'm worn out

You took my heart and tore it out
You tore it out of these hands
You're killing me slowly and
I don't understand, I don't understand

Chorus: Is this what they call love
I call it misery
Bittersweet
Is what's left of me

Is this what they call love
I call it misery
Bittersweet
Is what's left of me

I call it misery

This heart was only yours to hold
Oh why were you so cold
I wanted you to love me
But you just bring me down

These tired hands are reaching out
To help you find your way
But oh you take your pride in
Pushing me away, you're pushing me away

Chorus

Bridge: Everything ends I suppose this is true

Never did I think it was me and you
Reality sets in and dreams start to burst
But remember this one thing I loved you first

Chorus

"Misery"

11
1: to find a love that is worth mine but I'm tired and I'm worn out
Melody
Bm A2 G2
2: Piano
13
1: you took my heart and tore it out you tore it out of these
Melody
D2 A2
2: Piano
15
1: hands you're kill - ing me slow - ly and I don't un - der - stand
Melody
Bm A2 G2
2: Piano

17
1: I don't un - der - stand Is this what they call love
Melody
E7 G2 A2 D2
2: Piano
20
1: I call it mis - er - y bitt - er - sweet is what's left
Melody
A2 Bm A2 G2
2: Piano
22
1: of me Is this what they call love I call it mis - er - y
Melody
D2 A2
2: Piano

25
1: Melody
bitt - er - sweet is what's left of me
Bm
A2
G2
2: Piano
27
1: Melody
I call it mis - er - y
D2
A2
Bm
A2
G2
2: Piano
31
1: Melody
This heart was on - ly yours to hold
D2
2: Piano

Melody lyrics (m. 33): oh why were you so cold___ I want - ed you to love

Melody lyrics (m. 35): ___ me but you just bring me down___ These ti - red hands___ are reach -

Melody lyrics (m. 37): - ing out___ to help you find___ your way but oh you take pride___

39
1: Melody
in push - ing me a - way
you're push - ing me a - way
E7
2: Piano
41
1: Melody
Is this what they call love
I call it mis - er - y
G2 A2 D2 A2
2: Piano
44
1: Melody
bitt - er - sweet is what's left of me
Is this what they call love
Bm A2 G2 D2
2: Piano

47
1: Melody
I call it mis - er - y
bitt - er - sweet is what's left
A2 Bm A2 G2
2: Piano
49
1: Melody
of me
I call it mis - er - y
Em7 D/F♯ G
2: Piano
54
1: Melody
D/F♯ Em7 D C/E A
2: Piano

Ev - ery - thing ends____ I supp - ose____ this is true____

nev - er did I think____ it was me and you____ re -

al - i - ty____ sets in and dreams start to burst____ but re -

65
1: mem - ber this one thing I loved you first I loved you first
Melody
C/E Asus A Asus
2: Piano
69
1: Is this what they call love I call it mis - er - y
Melody
A D2 A2
2: Piano
72
1: bitt - er - sweet is what's left of me Is this what they call love
Melody
Bm A2 G2 D2
2: Piano

I call it mis - er - y ___ bitt - er - sweet is what's left ___

of me ___ I call it ___ mis - er - y

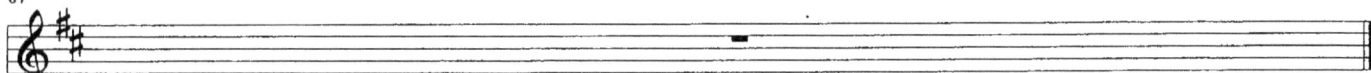

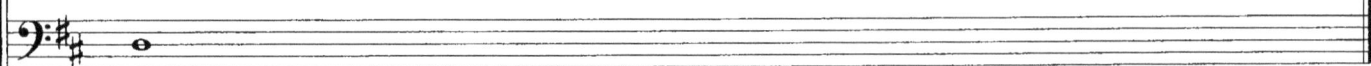

"DREAMER"

Lyrics by Christian Passen
Music by Wayne Bowers

There once was a boy with his head in the clouds
He didn't know then the things he knows now
He wore his heart on his black sweater sleeve
He had hopes that you wouldn't believe

The world would spin, it would be moved with laughter
Caught up in his dream, he lost sight of what he was after

Chorus: He saw the days pass
                  Love crashed on the shore
                  Love rained in his arms
                  Oh yes it did pour

                  He got to kiss lips
                  So ever divine
                  But while lost in his dream
                  He lost sight of time

                  And woke up alone
                  And woke up alone
                  And woke up alone
                  And woke up alone

He tried and he tried but he just couldn't win
Now he drowns his sorrows in a bottle of gin
He plays his guitar and sings about love
He sings about how it's never enough

He was called a fool, so much for trying
The faith he once had, is now slowly, slowing dying

Chorus

Bridge

He wanted to sleep and he wanted to dream
For reality is not what it seems
It comes with a pain that only heals if it scars
It comes with a voice that says who we are

She walked in, he gave all he once had
He was a sinking ship that wouldn't lift, lift up his flag

Chorus

Tag: He was a dreamer
             Oh he was a dreamer

"Dreamer"

Melody (m. 8): There once was a boy with his head in the clouds   He did - n't know then   the things

Melody (m. 12): he knows   now   He wore   his heart   on his   black sweat - er sleeve____   He had   hopes that   you

16
1: would - n't be - lieve___ The world would spin___ it would be moved with laugh - ter
Melo

G F G

2:
Piano

19
1: caught up in his dream He lost sight___ of what he was af - ter He saw the days pass love
Melo

F F/G G Am

2:
Piano

23
1: crashed on the shore___ love rained in his arms___ oh yes it did pour he got to kiss lips so
Melo

F2 Am

2:
Piano

27
1: ev - er di - vine but while lost in his dream he lost sight of time and woke up a - lone
Melo
G2
G
C
2:
Piano
31
1: and woke up a - lone and woke up a - lone and woke up a - lone
Melo
Am
C
2:
Piano
36
1: He tried and he tried but he just could - n't win now he
Melo
F
G
C
2:
Piano

40

1: drowns his sorrows in a bott - le of gin   he plays his gui - tar____ and sings   a - bout love   he
Melo

Am   C

2: Piano

44

1: sings   a - bout how____ it's nev - er e - nough   he was called   a fool____ so much____ for try - ing   the
Melo

F   G   F   G

2: Piano

48

1: faith he once had____ is now   slow - ly   slow - ly   dy - ing   He saw   the days   pass love
Melo

F   F/G   G   Am

2: Piano

52
1: crashed on the shore___ love rained in his arms___ oh yes it did pour he got to kiss lips so
Melo

F2   Am

2: Piano

56
1: ev - er di - vine___ but while lost in his dream___ he lost sight___ of time___ and woke up a - lone___
Melo

G2   G   A

2: Piano

60
1: ___ and woke up a - lone___   and woke up a - lone___
Melo

E/G#   A7/G   D2/F#   FMaj7

2: Piano

64

and woke up a-lone

Dm7   Esus   E   A   E/G#

69

He

A7/G   D2/F#   FMaj7   Dm7   Esus   E   D

75

want-ed to sleep___ and he want-ed to dream___ for re-al-i-ty is___ not what it seems it

C   Am

79

Melo: comes with a pain that on-ly heals if it scars it comes with a voice that says who we are

Piano: C   F   G

83

Melo: she walked in he gavve all he once had he was a sink-ing ship that would-n't lift lift

Piano: F   G   F   F/G

87

Melo: up his flag He saw the days pass love crashed on the shore___ love rained in his arms___ oh yes

Piano: G   Am   F2

91
1: it did pour he got to kiss lips so ev - er di - vine ___ but while lost in his dream ___ he lost
Melo
Am
G2
2:
Piano
95
Melo sight ___ of time ___ and woke up a - lone and woke up a - lone
G
C
Am
99
and woke up a - lone and woke up a - lone ___
Melo
C
F
G
Piano

104

He was a dream - er   oh he was a dream -
Melo

C   Am
Piano

107

- - - er   he was a dream - er
Melo

C
Piano

110

oh he was a dream - er____   He was a dream - er
Melo

F   G   C
Piano

114
1: oh he was a dream - - - - er he was a dream-
Melo
Am
C
2:
Piano
117
1: - er oh he was a dream - - er
Melo
F
G
2:
Piano

"TAKING FLIGHT"

Lyrics by Christian Passen
Music by Christian Passen & Wayne Bowers

Chorus: The city shines, what a sight
               I'm on a plane, taking flight

I talk to the stars about your grace
They answer back from space
Falling fast, onward down
Hoping I don't hit the ground

Chorus

My army of words, fell on down
To your response, I've found
You've hit me in ways, that I cannot describe
This war of love, I can't survive

Chorus

Bridge: I'll walk on forward, towards the light
               This time around I'll do things right
               Now I can see we weren't meant to be
               Now I can see, now I can see
               I raise my flag, I 'm giving up
               These feelings I have they can't be love

Chorus

Tag: I'm flying far, from my home
               But you're in my heart so I'm not alone

"Taking Flight"

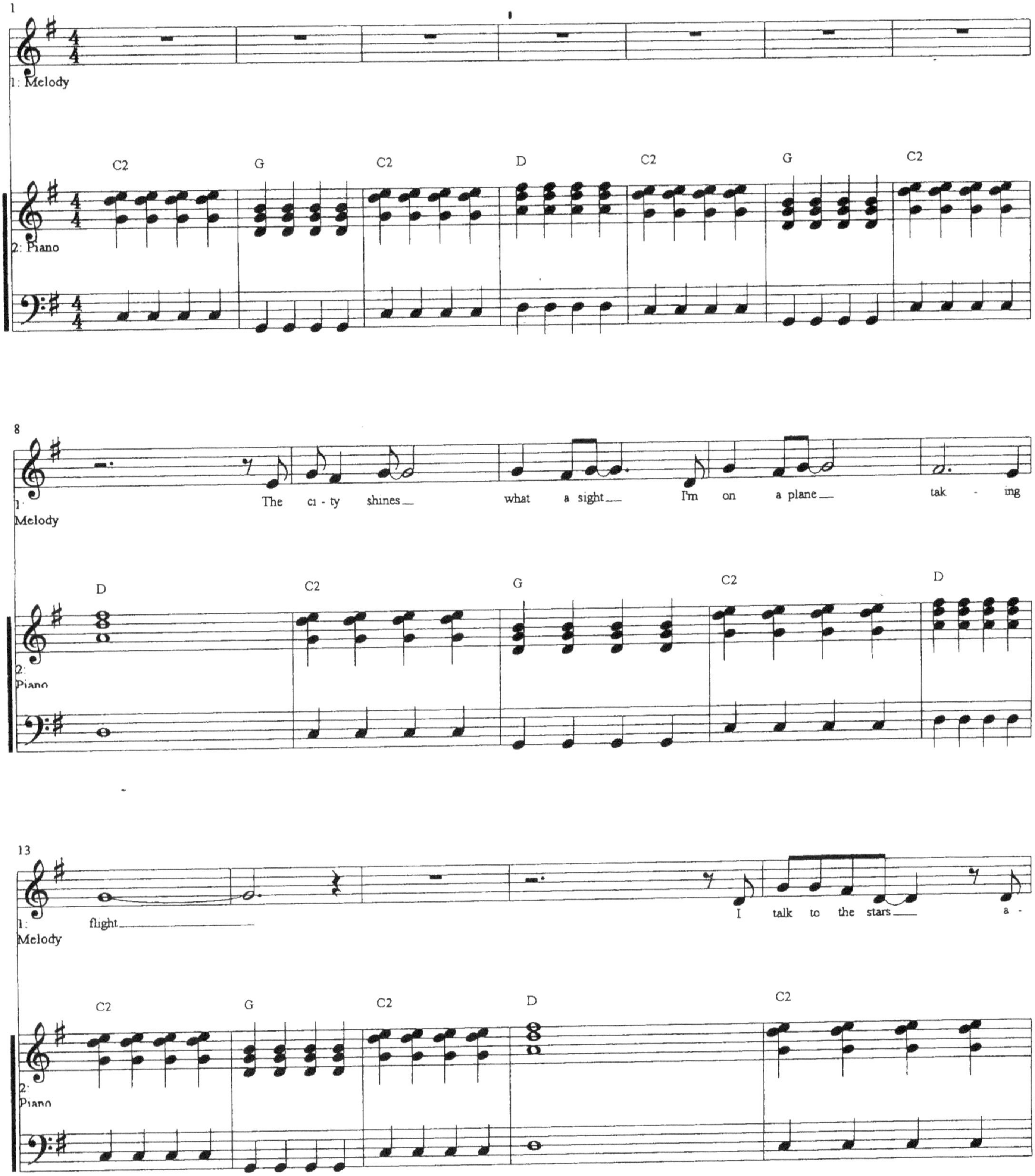

18

bout your grace they an - swer back____ from space fall - ing fast____

Melody

G   C2   D   C2

Piano

22

on - ward down____ hop - ing I____ don't hit the ground____

Melody

G   C2   D   C2

Piano

26

____ The ci - ty shines what a sight____ I'm

Melody

G   C2   D   C2   G

Piano

31
1: on a plane tak - ing flight My
Melody
C2 D C2 G C2 D
2: Piano
37
1: arm - y of words fell on down to your re - sponse I've found you've
Melody
C2 G C2 D
2: Piano
41
1: hit me in ways that I can - not des - cribe this war of love I can't sur - vive
Melody
C2 G C2 D C2
2: Piano

46
1: The ci - ty shines what a sight I'm
Melody
G C2 D C2 G
2: Piano
51
1: on a plane tak - ing flight I
Melody
C2 D C2 G C2 D
2: Piano
57
1: walk on for - ward towards the light this time a - round I'll do things right
Melody
G G/B Gsus/C Gsus/D Em7 Em7/D Dsus D/A
2: Piano

Now I can see____ we weren't meant____ to be now I can see____ now I can see____

I raise my flag____ I'm giv-ing up____ these

79

Melody: feel-ings I have___ they can't be love___

C2　　　　　　　　D　C2　　　　　G　C2

Piano

84

Melody: The ci-ty shines___ what a sight___ I'm on a plane___

D　　　　　　　　C2　　　　　G　　　　　C2

Piano

88

Melody: tak - ing I'm fly-ing far___ from my home___ but you're in my heart___ so I'm

D　　　　　　　　C2　　　　　G　　　　　C2

Piano

92
1: not a - lone I'm fly - ing far from my home but you're in my heart so I'm
Melody
D C2 G C2
2: Piano
96
1: not a - lone I'm fly - ing far from my home but you're in my heart so I'm
Melody
D C2 G C2
2: Piano
100
1: not a - lone I'm fly - ing far from my home but you're in my heart so I'm
Melody
D C2 G C2
2: Piano

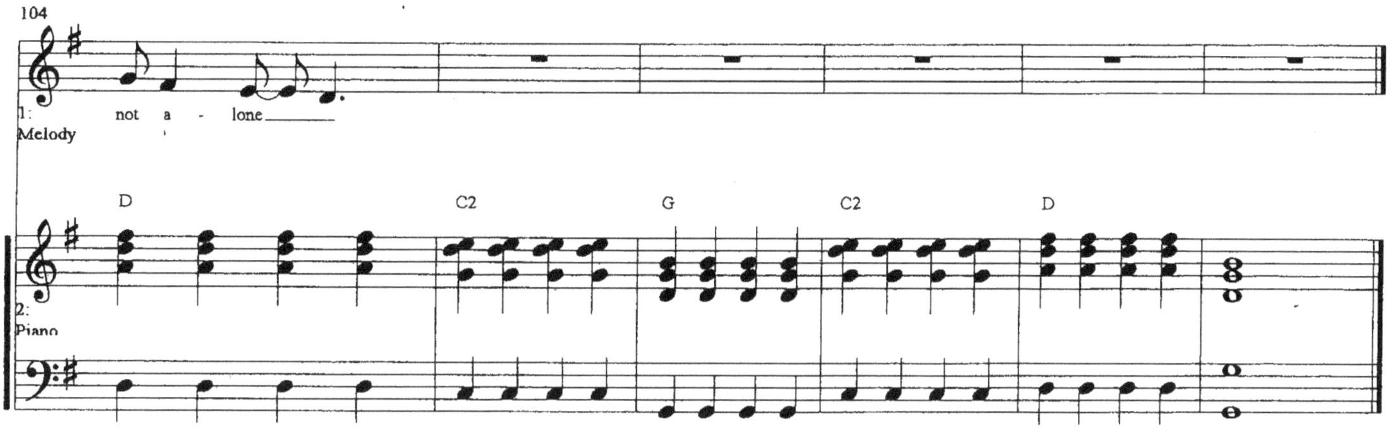
104
1:
not a - lone
Melody
D
C2
G
C2
D
2:
Piano

"DON'T LET ME DOWN"

Lyrics by Christian Passen
Music by Wayne Bowers

It's when I close my eyes
That all darkness fades
It's when I lift my hands
That the sun shines on my face

It's when I hear that song
That I think of you
It's when you leave my side
That I whisper I love you

I can feel it in my bones
Overwhelming like the sun
My arms are open wide
To embrace your love

Chorus: When I hold your hand I hold the world
           When I'm with you time means nothing
           When I see your face there's nothing else around
           When I kiss your lips my feet lift off the ground

           So don't let me down, don't let me down

I think it's safe to say
That everything's gonna be okay
I have a thousand words
But all I'm gonna say is

When I hear that song
That's when I think of you
It's when you leave my side
That I whisper I love you

I can feel it in my bones
Overwhelming like the sun

My arms are open wide
To embrace your love

Chorus

Bridge: Whoa oh oh, I'm still standing
               Whoa oh oh, I'm alive and well
               Whoa oh oh, can you understand

Chorus

Chorus

Tag: Don't let me down, whoa, whoa
           Don't let me down, whoa, whoa
           Don't let me down, whoa, whoa

"Don't Let Me Down"

Lyrics (melody line):

It's when I close my eyes ___
that all the dark - ness fades ___

It's when I lift my hands

that the sun shines on my face _____ It's

when I hear that song _____ that I think of you _____

It's when you leave my side____

that I whis-per I love you____ I can

feel it in my bones____ o - ver - whelm -

27

Melody: - ing like the sun_____ my

Am7
Piano

29

Melody: arms are o - pen wide_____ to em - brace_____ your

Em   Dsus
Piano

32

Melody: love   When I hold your hand_____ I hold the world_____

D   A   E
Piano

35

1: Melody _____ when I'm ____ with you time means

F#m   D   A   E   F#m
2: Piano

40

1: Melody no - - thing ____ when I see your face ____ there's

D   D2   A   E
2: Piano

43

1: Melody noth - ing else a - round ____ when I kiss your lips ____

F#m   D   A
2: Piano

46
1: Melody
my feet lift off the ground
E F♯m D C Bm Am
2: Piano
49
1: Melody
so don't let me down don't let me down
G C D G C Am D G C
2: Piano
55
1: Melody
I think it's safe to say that
D G C Dsus D G C D
2: Piano

60

1: ev - ery-thing's gonn - a be O K___ I have a thou - sand words___ but
Melody

G   C   Am   D   G   C   D

2: Piano

64

1: all I'm gonn - a say___ is when I hear that song___ that's when I think of you___
Melody

G   C   Am D G   C   D   G   C

2: Piano

69

1: It's when you leave my side___ that I whis-per I love
Melody

Am   D   G   C   D   G   C

2: Piano

73
1:
Melody
you I can feel it in my bones
Am D Em
2:
Piano
75
o - ver - whelm - - ing like the sun
Am7
77
my arms are o - pen wide
Em

80
1: Melody
to em - brace your love When I hold your hand
Dsus D A
2: Piano
83
1: Melody
I hold the world when I'm with
E F♯m D A
2: Piano
87
1: Melody
you time means no - - thing when I see your face
E F♯m D D2 A
2: Piano

91
1: Melody
there's noth - ing else a - round
when I kiss your lips
E
F♯m
D
A
2: Piano
95
1: Melody
my feet lift off the ground
E
F♯m
D C Bm Am
2: Piano
98
1: Melody
so don't let me down
don't let me down
C
D/B
Dm/B♭
A
2: Piano

103
1: Melo
Whoa I'm still stand - ing
C D/B Dm/B♭ A
2: Piano
107
whoa I'm a - live and well
C D/B Dm/B♭ A
111
whoa can you un - der - stand
C D/B Dm/B♭

115
1: Melody
When I hold your hand I hold the world
A
E
2: Piano
117
1: Melody
when I'm with you time means
F♯m
D
A
E
F♯m
2: Piano
122
1: Melody
no - - thing
when I see your face
there's
D
D2
A
E
2: Piano

125
1: Melody
noth - ing else a - round
when I kiss your lips
F♯m
D
A
E
2: Piano
129
1: Melody
When I hold your hand
I hold the world
A
E
2: Piano
131
1: Melody
when I'm
with you
time means
F♯m
D
A
E
F♯m
2: Piano

136

1: Melody no - - thing_____ when I see your face_____ there's

D D2 A E

2: Piano

139

1: Melody noth - ing else a - round_____ when I kiss your lips_____

F#m D A

2: Piano

142

1: Melody _____ my feet lift off the ground_____

E F#m D C Bm Am

2: Piano

145
1: Melody
so don't let me down
don't let me down
G C D G C Am D
2: Piano
150
1: Melody
Don't let me down
whoa
whoa
Don't let me down
G C D G C Am D G C
2: Piano
155
1: Melody
whoa
whoa
Don't let me down
whoa
D G C Am D G C D G C
2: Piano

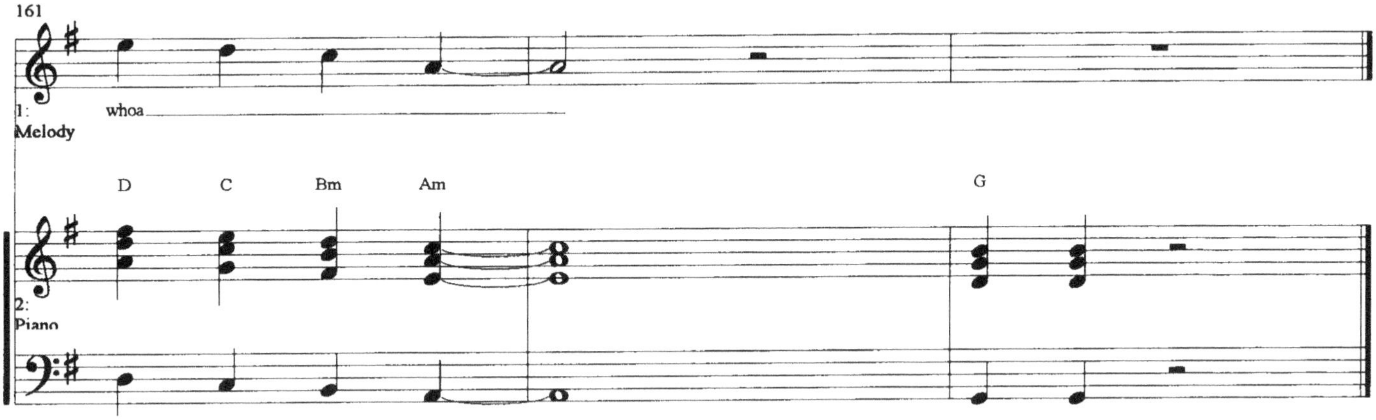
161
1:
whoa
Melody
D
C
Bm
Am
G
2:
Piano

"WHY IS IT I"

Lyrics by Christian Passen
Music by Wayne Bowers

We're running forward now
And leaving behind
The doors of our future
I thought you were mine

You're running from something
But I'm lost in the nothing
And I am wanting now
So much more

I wanted your love
I wanted your touch
I wanted to hold you
Oh so much

Chorus: Why is it I
            Who sits here alone
            Lost in the moments
            That made you feel close

            Why is it I
            Who sits here alone
            Lost in this quest
            To Find my way home

            Oh why is it I

It feels like you're falling
You're fading away
While I am stuck begging
I'm starting to pray

I need you here
Tell me what it will take

I'm hurting without you
Can I get you to stay

It doesn't feel right
To not have you close
I need you to hear me
So please don't let go

Chorus

Bridge: So if you decide
            To stay here tonight
            And give me a chance
            To make things right

            I promise I'll be
            All that you need
            There wont be a reason
            To let go of me

Chorus

"WHY IS IT I"

We're runn - ing for - ward now and leav-ing be - hind

the doors of our fu-ture I thought you were mine

32
1: You're runn - ing from some - thing but I'm lost in the noth - ing
Melo
Am G/B C F2
2:
Piano
40
1: and I am want - ing now so much more I want -
Melo
Am G/B C F2 Dm7
2:
Piano
50
1: ed your love I want-ed your touch I want - ed to
Melo
G/B Dm7
2:
Piano

hold you _____ oh so much _____ Why is it I _____ who sits here a-

lone lost in the mom - ents that made you feel _____ close why is it I _____ who

sits here a - lone lost in this quest to find my way _____ home why is it I _____

81

Melo: who sits here a - lone lost in the mom - ents that made you feel____ close

Piano: C   Am7   F2   G

88

Melo: why is it I_____ who sits here a - lone lost in this quest to find my way____

Piano: C   Am7   F2

95

Melo: home_____ oh why is it I_____

Piano: G   Am G/B C   F2

104

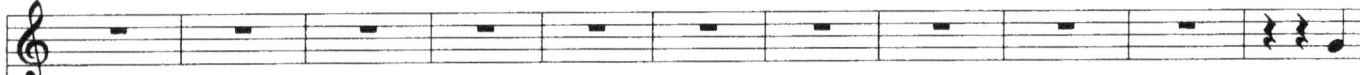

It

115

feels   like   you're fall - ing you're fad - ing a - way_____   while   I   am   stuck   begg - ing   I'm

126

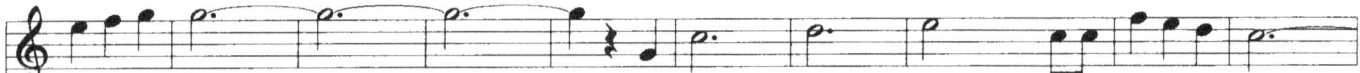

start - ing   to   pray_____   I   need   you   here   tell me   what it will   take_____

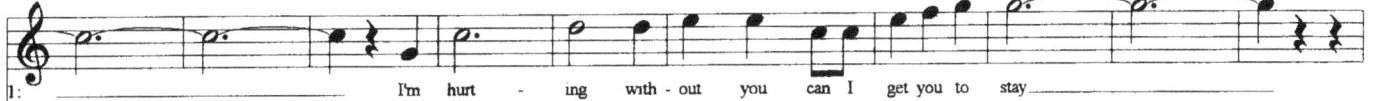

164
1: sits here a - lone lost in the mom - ents that made you feel close why is it I
Melo
Am7
F2
G
2:
Piano
171
1: who sits here a - lone lost in this quest to find my way home
Melo
C
Am7
F2
G
2:
Piano
178
1: why is it I who sits here a - lone lost in the mom - ents that
Melo
C
Am7
F2
2:
Piano

8

206
1:
Melo
so
C6
2:
Piano
213
1: if you de - cide to stay here to - night
Melo
B♭Maj7
C6
2:
Piano
220
1: and give me a chance to make things right
Melo
B♭Maj7
C6
2:
Piano

228
1: I prom - ise I'll be all that you
Melo

BbMaj7 C6

2: Piano

235
1: need there wont be a rea - son to let
Melo

BbMaj7 C6

2: Piano

242
1: go of me to let go of me
Melo

D2

2: Piano

248
1: Why is it I who sits here a - lone lost in the mom - ents that
Melo
C
Am7
F2
2:
Piano
254
1: made you feel close why is it I who sits here a - lone lost in this
Melo
G
C
Am7
2:
Piano
261
1: quest to find my way home why is it I who sits here a - lone
Melo
F2
G
C
Am7
2:
Piano

268

1: lost in the mom - ents that made you feel _____ close why is it I _____ who
Melo

F2   G   C

2: Piano

274

1: sits here a - lone lost in this quest to find my way___ home _____ oh
Melo

Am7   F2   G

2: Piano

282

1: why is it I _____
Melo

Am   G/B   C   F2   Am

2: Piano

"REFLECTIONS"

Lyrics by Christian Passen
Music by Wayne Bowers

Baby why must you scream
Can't you see I'm trying to sleep
You mean so much to me
If only you weren't a dream

If you were here with me
I'd kiss your lips so sweet
If I could hold you now
I'd never let you go

Chorus: This life is a broken mirror
              All I see are reflections
              What is, what was
              And what will never be

              Oh why won't it be
              Don't tell me that
              Love is just a dream
              Oh love is just a dream

              Trapped inside of me

I would hold you so very tight
Tell you how life would turn out right
Oh baby turn off the light
'Cause it's time to say goodnight

You follow each lonely step
And mock every last regret
And I'd be willing to bet
That you aren't finished yet

Chorus

Bridge: It's a one sided love
                 And I just can't let go
                 It's a blind sided pain
                 One of which you did not know

                 You couldn't see me
                 Down upon my knees
                 Beggin' for your love
                 Was it just not enough

Chorus

Tag: I thought I should tell you
                 I thought I should say
                 That life is much harder
                 When you are awake

"Reflections"

Ba - by why must you scream___ can't you see___ I'm try-ing to sleep___ you

mean so much to me___ if on - ly you weren't a dream___

13
1: Melody — If you were here with me____ I'd kiss your lips so sweet____

Eb   Bb
2: Piano

15
1: Melody — if I could hold you now____ I'd nev-er let you go____ This

Cm   Bb
2: Piano

17
1: Melody — life is a bro-ken mirr-or all I see____ are re-flec-tions what is____

Cm   Bb
2: Piano

19
1: Melody
what was and what will nev - er be Oh
AbMaj7
Bb
2: Piano
21
1: Melody
why wont it be don't tell me that love is just a dream
Cm
Bb
2: Piano
23
1: Melody
oh love is just a dream trapped in-side of me
AbMaj7
Bb
Eb
2: Piano

26
1: Melody
Bb Cm Bb Eb Bb Cm
2: Piano
32
1: Melody
I would hold you so ve - ry tight tell you how life
Bb Eb
2: Piano
34
1: Melody
would turn out right oh
Bb
2: Piano

35
1: Melody
bab - y turn off the light 'cause it's
Cm
2: Piano
36
1: Melody
time to say good-night you foll-ow each lone - ly step and
B♭
E♭
2: Piano
38
1: Melody
mock ev-ery last re-gret and I'd be will-ing to bet that
B♭
Cm
2: Piano

40

1: Melody you aren't fin-ished yet This life is a bro-ken mirr - or

Bb   Cm

2: Piano

42

1: Melody all I see___ are re-flec - tions what is___ what was___ and what will

Bb   AbMaj7

2: Piano

44

1: Melody nev - er be___ Oh why wont it be___ don't

Bb   Cm

2: Piano

46

1: Melody tell me that_____ love is just_____ a dream_____ oh love is just_____ a dream_____

2: Piano

Bb   AbMaj7

48

1: Melody _____ trapped in-side_____ of me_____

2: Piano

Bb   Gm   F   EbMaj7   F

53

1: Melody   It's a

2: Piano

Gm   F   EbMaj7   F

57

1: Melody one side - ed love____ and I just____ can't let go____ it's a blind____

Gm F

2: Piano

59

1: Melody ____ side - ed pain____ one of which____ you did not____

EbMaj7 F

2: Piano

61

1: Melody you could-n't see me____ down up - on____ my knees____

Gm F

2: Piano

63
1: Melody
begg-ing for your love
was it just not e-nough
Eb Maj7
F
2: Piano
65
1: Melody
This
Gsus
G
F
2: Piano
67
1: Melody
life is a bro - ken mirr - or
all I see are re-flec - tions what is
Cm
Bb
2: Piano

69
1: Melody
what was and what will nev - er be Oh
AbMaj7
Bb
2: Piano
71
1: Melody
why wont it be don't tell me that love is just a dream
Cm
Bb
2: Piano
73
1: Melody
oh love is just a dream trapped in-side of me
AbMaj7
Bb
Eb
2: Piano

Melody lyrics, measure 79: thought I should tell _____ you I thought _____

Melody lyrics, measure 80: _____ I should say _____ that

81

1: Melody — life is much hard - er when you are a-wake__ I

2: Piano — Cm / B♭

83

1: Melody — thought I should tell_____ you I thought_____

2: Piano — E♭

84

1: Melody — I should say_____ that

2: Piano — B♭

85

1: Melody — life is much hard - er when you are a-wake_____ I

Cm   Bb
2: Piano

87

1: Melody — thought I should tell____ you I thought____ I should say____ that life____

Eb   Bb
2: Piano

89

1: Melody ____ is much hard - er when you are a-wake___

Cm   Bb
2: Piano

91

1: Melody

E♭

2: Piano

"INCOMPLETE"

Lyrics by Christian Passen
Music by Wayne Bowers

I look around and wish that
I was someone else
Why am I never satisfied
Being myself

I step back and look at
All the things I've done
Hey dad are you
Proud of your son

Chorus: I'm broken glass upon a dusty floor
      Tell me what you see and I'll show you more
      Beyond this face and past this heart
      It's Incomplete, but It's a start

I lived the dream of man and found
An everlasting love
I guess the dreams of my time
Didn't quite make the cut

I learned to lose but I know
That I am still learning
Hey God, how is the world
How is it still turning

Chorus

Bridge: There's a will inside I can't explain
     Maybe that is why I accept the pain
     Love was lost and this heart got jaded
     The smile I once knew quickly faded

I fell asleep and I lived
Another lonely night

Please tell me that I've done
At least one thing right

I can't take the fire
I'll burn just the same
I know that I am
I am the one to blame

Chorus

Chorus

"Incomplete"

Lyrics:

I look a-round and wish that I was some-one else

why am I nev-er sat-is-fied be-ing my-self I step back and

18
1: look at all the things I've done hey dad
Melody
D Asus/D D Dsus Asus/D D Dsus
2: Piano
22
1: are you proud of your son I'm brok - en glass up -
Melody
D Asus/D D Dsus Asus/D Bm G
2: Piano
26
1: on a dust - y floor tell me what you see and I'll show you more be - yond this face and
Melody
A Bm G Bm A Bm G
2: Piano

30
1: Melody
past this heart it's in - com - plete but it's a start
A Bm Bm A D Dsus D Asus/D D Dsus
2: Piano
36
1: Melody
I lived the dream of
Asus/D D Dsus D Asus/D D Dsus Asus/D D Dsus
2: Piano
42
1: Melody
man and found an ev - er - last - ing love I guess the dreams
D Asus/D D Dsus Asus/D D Dsus
2: Piano

46
1: of my time did - n't quite make the cut I learned to lose
Melody
D Asus/D D Dsus Asus/D D Dsus
2: Piano
50
1: but I know that I am still learn_____ ing Hey God how is the world how
Melody
D Asus/D D Dsus Asus/D D Dsus D Asus/D
2: Piano
55
1: is it still turn - ing I'm brok - en glass up - on a dust - y floor tell me what you see and I'll
Melody
D Dsus Asus/D Bm G A Bm G
2: Piano

60
1: show you more be - yond this face and past this heart it's in - com - plete
Melody
Bm A Bm G A Bm Bm A
2: Piano
64
1: but it's a start
Melody
Em D/F♯ Em7 D Em D/F♯
2: Piano
71
1:
Melody
G Asus A Em D/F♯ Em7 D Em D/F♯
2: Piano

79
1:
Melody
There's a will inside
I can't explain
G Asus A Em D/F# Em7 D
2: Piano
85
may - be that is why
I ac - cept the pain
Love was lost
Em D/F# G Asus A Em
90
and this heart
got ja - ded
the smile I once knew
D/F# Em7 D Em D/F#

95

quick - ly fad - ed___ I fell a-sleep and I lived a - noth-er lone-ly

Melody

G   Asus   A   D   Dsus   D   Asus/D   D   Dsus

Piano

100

night   please tell me that   I've done   at least   one thing   right   I   can't

Melody

Asus/D   D   Dsus   D   Asus/D   D   Dsus   Asus/D   D   Dsus

Piano

106

take   the fire   I'll burn   just the same   I know   that   I   am   I am the one to

Melody

D   Asus/D   D   Dsus   Asus/D   D   Dsus   D   Asus/D   D   Dsus

Piano

112

Melody: blame_____ I'm brok - en glass up - on a dust - y floor tell me what you see and I'll

Asus/D   Bm   G   A   Bm   G

116

Melody: show you more____ be - yond this face and past this heart it's in - com - plete____

Bm   A   Bm   G   A   Bm   Bm   A

120

Melody: ____ I'm brok - en glass up - on a dust - y floor tell me what you see and I'll

Bm   G   A   Bm   G

124
1: show you more be - yond this face and past this heart it's in - com - plete
Melody
Bm A Bm G A Bm Bm A
2: Piano
128
1: but it's a start
Melody
D Dsus D Asus/D D Dsus Asus/D D Dsus D Asus/D
2: Piano
135
1:
Melody
D Dsus Asus/D D
2: Piano

"HOW IT HAS TO BE"

Lyrics by Christian Passen
Music by Wayne Bowers

Intro: I can't explain this feeling
    It's one I haven't felt before
    I was drowning in love
    And I couldn't ask for more

    But then something happened
    That I cannot explain
    But now when I see you
    My heart fills with pain

How can you stand there
With hate in your eyes
Why can't you just forgive me
And accept my goodbye

I left for a reason
Though you choose not to see
The love that we shared
It brought me to my knees

Chorus: It's killing me now
    How I wish you could see
    This isn't what I wanted
    But it's how it has to be

You say you are drowning
In all the tears you've cried
You whisper so softly
Has our love truly died

I try not to answer
Because I know that you know the truth
This heart has been shattered
And it's all thanks to you

Chorus

Bridge: My life has a darkness
There's an evil in my soul
But there's a light in the distance
A place which you can't go

This wasn't my choice
You asked to stay behind
I wanted so badly
To someday call you mine

Chorus

"How It Has To Be"

Lyrics:

1: Melody — I can't ex-plain this feel-ing __ it's one I have-n't felt be-fore __

Melody — I was drown-ing in love __ and I could-n't ask for more __

Melody — But then some-thing happ-ened __ that I can-not ex-plain __

13

Melody: But now when I see___ you___ my heart fills with pain___

Piano chords: Dm C B♭ Gm Dm C Gm B♭

17

Melody

Piano chords: F C B♭ F C Gm B♭ F C B♭

23

Melody: How can you stand there___

Piano chords: F C Gm B♭ Dm C B♭ Gm

28 with hate in your eyes_____ why can't you just for - give me_____

32 and ac - cept my good - bye_____ I left for a rea - son_____

36 though you choose not to see_____ The love that we shared it

4

brought me to my knees_____ It's kill-ing me now_____

1:
Melody

Dm   C Gm   Bb   F   C Bb

2:
Piano

how I wish you could see_____ This is-n't what I want - ed____

1:
Melody

F   C Gm   Bb   F   C Bb

2:
Piano

but it's how it has   to be_____ It's kill-ing me now_____

1:
Melody

F   C Gm   Bb   F   C Bb

2:
Piano

53

Melody: how I wish you could see _____ This is-n't what I want-ed

Piano chords: F C Gm Bb F C Bb

57

Melody: but it's how it has to be _____ How it has to be _____

Piano chords: F C Gm Bb Dm C Bb

61

Melody: how it has to be _____

Piano chords: Gm Dm C Gm Bb Dm C Bb Gm

66
Melody: You say you are drown - ing

Piano: Dm C Gm B♭ Dm C B♭ Gm

71
Melody: in all the tears you've cried ____ you whis - per so soft - ly ____

Piano: Dm C Gm B♭ Dm C B♭ Gm

75
Melody: has our love tru - ly died ____ I try not to an - swer ____

Piano: Dm C Gm B♭ Dm C B♭ Gm

because I know that you know the truth___ This heart has been shatt - ered___

and it's all thanks to you___ It's kill - ing me now___

how I wish you could see___ This is - n't what I want - ed___

92
1:
Melody
but it's how it has to be
It's kill - ing me now
F C Gm B♭ F C B♭
2:
Piano
96
how I wish you could see
This is - n't what I want - ed
F C Gm B♭ F C B♭
100
but it's how it has to be
My life has a dark - ness
there's an
F C Gm B♭ Gm7 C/G

105

e - vil in my soul_____ but there's a light in the dis - tance_____ a

Gm7   A/G   Gm7   C/G

109

place which you can't go_____ This was - n't my choice_____ you

Gm7   A/G   Gm7   C/G

113

asked to stay___ be-hind_____ I want-ed so bad - ly___ to some - day call you mine.

Gm7   A/G   Gm7   C/G   Gm7

118
1:
Melody
to call you mine
A Dm C B♭ Gm Dm C Gm B♭
2:
Piano
123
1:
Melody
It's kill-ing me now
Dm C B♭ Gm Dm C Gm B♭ F C B♭
2:
Piano
129
1:
Melody
how I wish you could see
This is-n't what I want - ed
F C Gm B♭ F C B♭
2:
Piano

134
1: Melody
but it's how it has to be
It's kill - ing me now
F C Gm B♭ F C B♭
2: Piano
138
1: Melody
how I wish you could see
This is - n't what I want - ed
F C Gm B♭ F C B♭
2: Piano
142
1: Melody
but it's how it has to be
How it has to be
F C Gm B♭
2: Piano

"SAFETY NET"

Lyrics by Christian Passen
Music by Eric Daugherty & Wayne Bowers

I met her by the bridge
Right before she wished to fall
And I said Darling take a moment and listen
To what I have to say

And she said
I've thought this over and over
I don't want to think it over again
Over again

We'll jump together, we won't fall at all
Despite what other people say
We'll rise above the darkness
We won't let it get in our way

Chorus: And I said, I know you barely know me
             And I'm aware that we just met
             But honey, there's a whole world out there
             And if you'd ask me to be your safety net, I would be

I swear I saw a tear in her eye
We held each other and cried
'Cause sometimes it's all that we can do
When you feel like it is goodbye

And she said with heartfelt eyes
For what reason do you stay
And I said to her with utmost compassion
More reasons than to walk away

We'll jump together, we won't fall at all
Despite what other people say
We'll rise above the darkness
We won't let it get in our way

Chorus

Bridge: I would be anything you want me to be
Anything at all so baby please
Say that we'll make it through it all
That we'll stand together, that we'll be strong

I will do anything you want me to do
Anything at all with only you
Say that we'll make it through the storm
That we'll stand together, that we've been reborn

Chorus

"Safety Net"

1: Melody
2: Piano
B EMaj7 B F#add4 G#m7
I met her by the
EMaj7 B F#add4 B
bridge right be - fore she wished to fall and I said
EMaj7 B F#add4

14

1: Melody — dar - ling take a mom - ent and list-en to what I have to say___ and she

G#m7 EMaj7 B F#add4

2: Piano

18

1: Melody — said___ I've thought this___ o - ver and o - ver___ I don't

B EMaj7 B

2: Piano

21

1: Melody — want to think it o - ver a - gain___ o - ver a -

F#add4 G#m7 EMaj7 B

2: Piano

25

1: Melody
gain _____ we'll jump to - geth - er we wont fall at all des - pite what

F#add4   EMaj7   F#add4

2: Piano

29

1: Melody
o - ther peo - ple say we'll rise a - bove the dark - ness we wont

EMaj7

2: Piano

32

1: Melody
let it get in our way and I said _____ I know you ___ bare - ly

F#Maj7   G#m7   EMaj7

2: Piano

36
1: Melody
know me ___ and I'm a - ware that we just met but hon - ey ___ there's a
B
F#add4
G#m7
EMaj7
2: Piano
40
1: Melody
whole world. out there ___ and if you'd ask me to be ___
B
F#add4
EMaj7
2: Piano
43
1: Melody
your safe - ty net ___ I would be
F#add4
B
EMaj7
2: Piano

48
1: Melody
B
F#add4
G#m7
EMaj7
B
2: Piano
53
1: Melody
I swear I saw a tear in her eye we held each o-ther and
F#add4
B
EMaj7
B
2: Piano
58
1: Melody
cried 'cause some-times it's all that we can do when you
F#add4
G#m7
EMaj7
2: Piano

feel like it is _____ good - bye _____ and she said _____ with heart - felt _____ eyes for what

B   F#add4   B   EMaj7

rea - son _____ do you stay   and I said   to her   with ut -

B   F#add4   G#m7

- most com - pass - ion   more rea - sons   than to walk   a - way

EMaj7   B   F#add4

we'll jump to - geth - er   we wont fall   at   all   des - pite   what

EMaj7   F#add4

o - ther peo - ple say   we'll rise   a - bove   the dark - ness   we wont

EMaj7

let it get in our way   and I said _____   I know you ___ bare - ly

F#Maj7   G#m7   EMaj7

know me and I'm a-ware that we just met but hon-ey there's a

whole world out there and if you'd ask me to be

your safe-ty net I would be an-y-thing you

92
1: Melody
want me to be an - y - thing at all so ba - by please
EMaj7
B
F#add4
2: Piano
95
1: Melody
say that we'll make it through it all that we'll stand to-geth - er that we'll be strong
B
EMaj7
B
F#add4
2: Piano
99
1: Melody
I would do an - y - thing you want me to do an - y - thing at all
B
EMaj7
B
2: Piano

102
1: Melody
with on - ly you say that we'll make it through the storm that we'll stand to - geth - er that
F♯add4 B EMaj7 B
2: Piano
106
1: Melody
we've been re - born and I said I know you bare - ly
F♯add4 G♯m7 EMaj7
2: Piano
110
1: Melody
know me and I'm a - ware that we just met but hon - ey there's a
B F♯add4 G♯m7 EMaj7
2: Piano

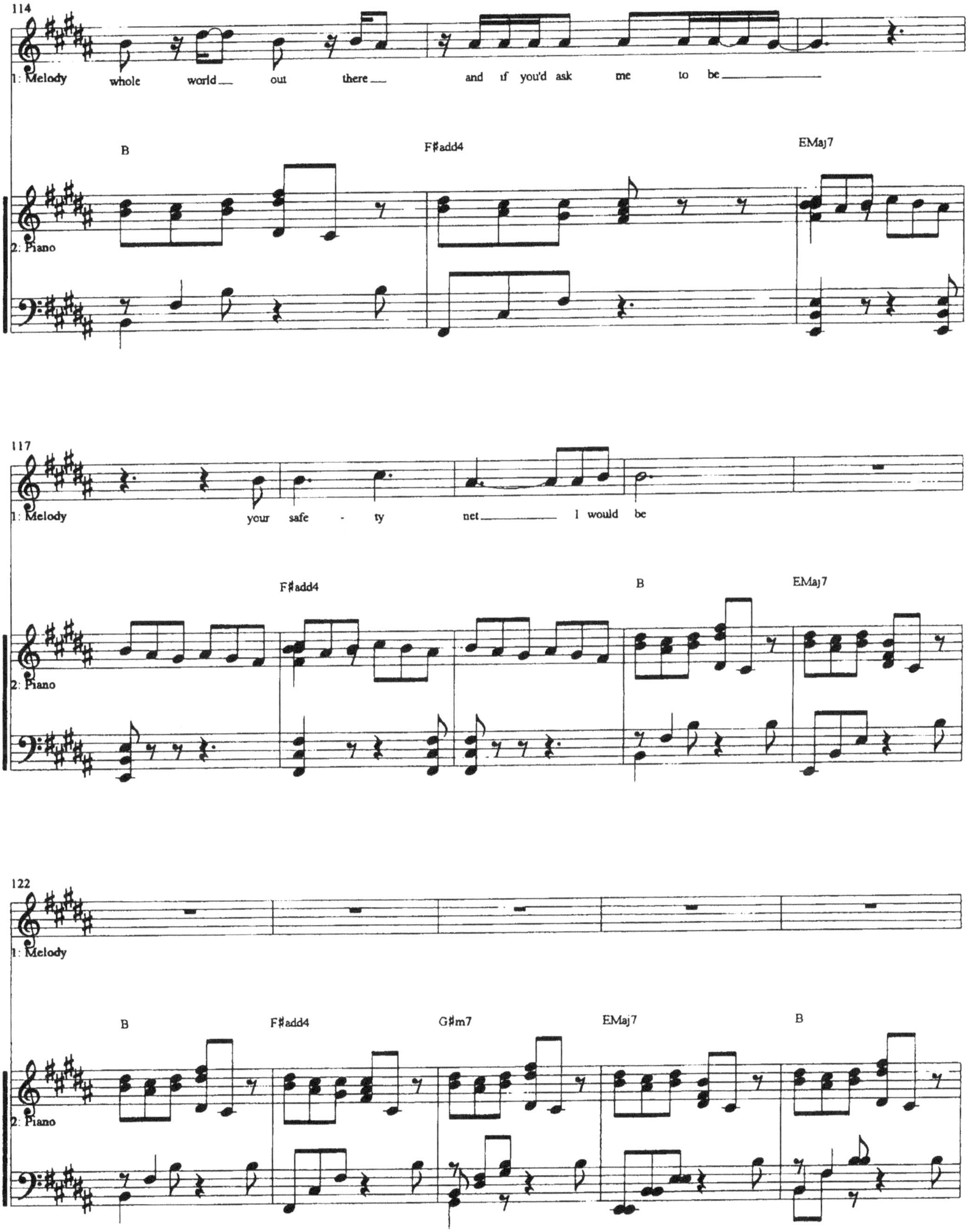

Lyrics (Melody line):

whole world out there and if you'd ask me to be

your safe - ty net I would be

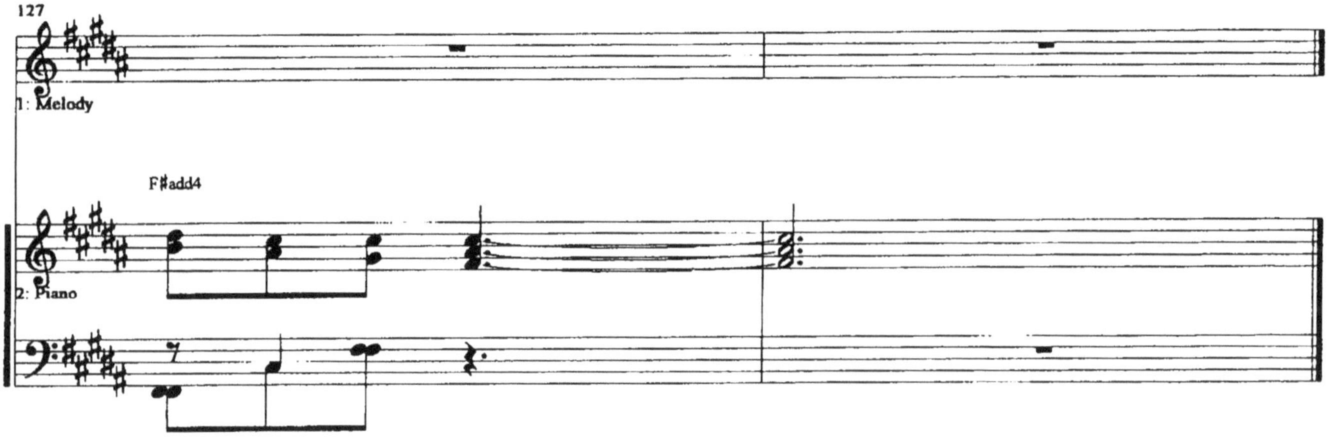
127
1: Melody
F#add4
2: Piano

"TEMPORARY"

Lyrics by Christian Passen
Music by Wayne Bowers

Look at this man, he's so confused
Some say he's crazy, some say that he's bruised
He runs from his past, He runs towards his home
He runs from himself and finds he's alone

He searches for love, upon the other side
He knows she isn't there, but his love has not died
He strives for a dream, a love that is true
The love he now knows is not what he knew

He walks away in silence
Leaves his footprints behind
He's torn between the path of his heart
And the chaos in his mind

Chorus: Oh break me down
               I'm too weak to stand
               Is this what it means
               Is this what it means
               To be a man?

               The darkness within
               It is changing me
               But the faith I have
               The faith I have
               It lets me see

               It's Temporary

Tears start to fall, from his saddened eyes
He starts to pray, and he looks to the sky
Tell me what is wrong, and what is right
Give me the strength to get through this night

Looking to the sky, he wishes to return
His past is in the fire, just watch it burn
Filled with so much hate, only towards himself
He's the one to blame the fault's with no one else

He walks away in silence
Leaves his footprints behind
He's torn between the path of his heart
And the chaos in his mind

Chorus

Bridge: Running down the road he screams, "I am free"
After all the years the crazy one is he
So here he resides in this darkness alone
Lost in his mind his future's unknown

Chorus

"TEMPORARY"

Look at this man____ he's so con-fused some say he's cra - zy some say____ that he's bruised____ he runs____ from his past____ he runs____ towards his home____ he runs____

15
1: Melody
from him - self and finds he's a - lone he search - es for love up - on the
B♭7
E♭m
2: Piano
18
1: Melody
oth - er side he knows she is - n't there but his love has not died he strives for a dream a love
A♭m
E♭m
2: Piano
22
1: Melody
that is true the love he now knows is not what he knew He
B♭7
2: Piano

25 Melody: walks a - way in si - lence leaves his foot - prints be - hind he's

Piano: Fm Eb

29 Melody: torn be - tween the path of his heart and the cha - os in his mind

Piano: Fm Gm Ab Bb

33 Melody: Oh break me down I'm too weak to stand is this what it means

Piano: Cm Bb Ab Eb

37
1: Melody
is this what it means to be a man the
Cm
Bb
Ab
Bb
2: Piano
41
1: Melody
dark - ness with - in it is chang - - - ing me but the faith I have
Cm
Bb
Ab
Eb
2: Piano
45
1: Melody
the faith I have it lets me see it's temp - or - ary -
Cm
Bb
Ab
Bb
2: Piano

50
1: Melody
y
E♭m
A♭m
E♭m
2: Piano
56
1: Melody
Tears start to fall from his sad-ened eyes he starts
B♭7
E♭m
2: Piano
60
1: Melody
to pray and he looks to the sky tell me what is wrong and what is right
A♭m
E♭m
2: Piano

64
1: Melody
give me the strength to get through this night Look - ing to the sky he wish - es
B♭7
E♭m
2: Piano
67
1: Melody
to re - turn his past is in the fire just watch it burn filled with so much hate on - ly
A♭m
E♭m
2: Piano
71
1: Melody
towards him - self he's the one to blame the fault's with no one else He
B♭7
2: Piano

74

1: Melody walks a - way ____ in si - lence leaves his foot - prints be - hind he's

Fm   E♭

2: Piano

78

1: Melody torn be - tween ____ the path of his heart ____ and the cha - os in ____ his mind ____

Fm   Gm   A♭   B♭

2: Piano

82

1: Melody Oh break me down ____ I'm too weak ____ to stand ____ is this what it means ____

Cm   B♭   A♭   E♭

2: Piano

86 — 1: Melody _____ is this what it means _____ to be _____ a man _____ the

2: Piano — Cm — Bb — Ab — Bb

90 — 1: Melody dark - ness with - in _____ it is chang - - ing me _____ but the faith I have _____

2: Piano — Cm — Bb — Ab — Eb

94 — 1: Melody _____ the faith I have _____ it lets _____ me see _____ it's temp - or - ary -

2: Piano — Cm — Bb — Ab — Bb

99
1: Melody
- y
B A2 B A2/E B A2 B
2: Piano
106
1: Melody
Runn-ing down the road he screams
I am free
F♯sus F♯ B A2 B
2: Piano
110
1: Melody
af - ter all the years the cra - zy one is he
A2/E B A2 B
2: Piano

so here he re - sides in this dark-ness a - lone

lost in his mind his fu - ture's un - known un - known

Oh break me down I'm too weak to stand is this what it means

128
1: Melody
is this what it means to be a man the
Cm Bb Ab Bb
2: Piano
132
1: Melody
dark - ness with - in it is chang - - - - ing me but the faith I have
Cm Bb Ab Eb
2: Piano
136
1: Melody
the faith I have it lets me see it's temp - or - ary -
Cm Bb Ab Bb
2: Piano

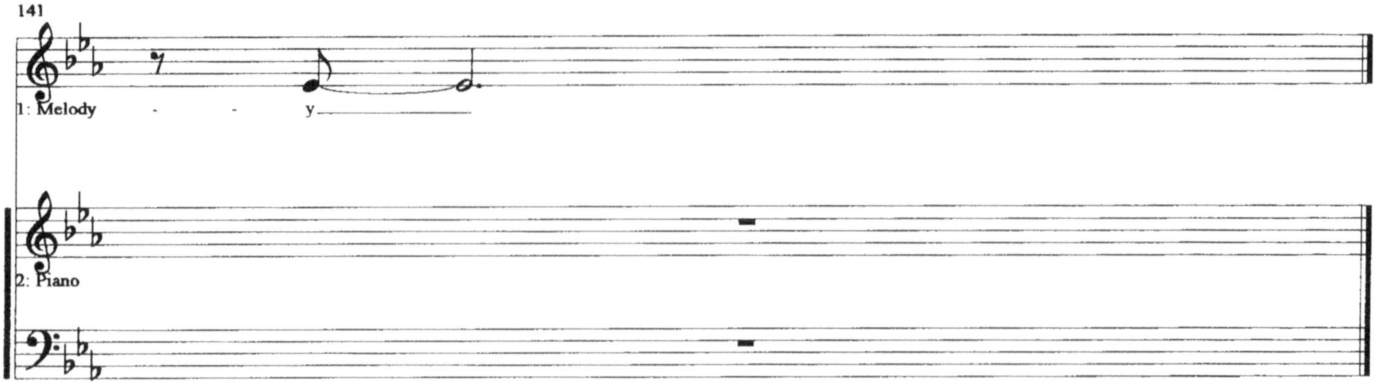
141
1: Melody
- - y
2: Piano

(END)

www.ingramcontent.com/pod-product-compliance
Lightning Source LLC
Chambersburg PA
CBHW081514040426
42447CB00013B/3218